WOMEN WITH CON HUSBAND

Making Sense of a Controlling Husband-What every woman must know

EMILY WALKER

2

INTRODUCTION

In this book about a controlling husband, I'm going to assume that you have already determined that you're in a relationship with a controlling, abusive man. You've probably known for a while that something wasn't right, but you couldn't put your finger on what was wrong. However, your suspicions were recently confirmed that you are not the problem, but he is, despite him blaming you for everything for years.

You can probably tell that the wonderful person you fell for the first time is not the man you are now married to. You can now see some of the indications of a controlling spouse. You realize that he was controlling your time, your outfits, your diet, your finances, your relationships with friends and family, and your children. By belittling and criticizing you he was controlling your thoughts, beliefs and your decision making.

He was also clearly controlling your emotions. He can make you feel awful just by the way he talks to you, or by using a certain tone of voice or a certain look. He also knows how to make you feel good, but somehow nowadays that does not happen very often. Then there's the drama and chaos, the crisis and problems that wreak havoc on your emotions and keep you running from one end of the day to the other, leaving you physically exhausted with no time to rest or think.

If you've ever thought you were going insane because you couldn't make sense of what was going on in your relationship, or if you think things would be so much better if he would just stop doing certain things and treat you nicely, this book is for you. And if you're perplexed as to how someone you love can be so cruel and heartless to you, keep reading.

The Nature Of A Controlling Husband

You probably wouldn't have started a relationship with your controlling husband if you knew what you know now. He knows that, too, and he also knows how to conceal his true nature from you at first, so you don't have all the information you need to make an informed decision about getting into a relationship with him. To put it another way, you were tricked. He purposefully withheld information and presented you with false information about himself in order to make you believe he would be an excellent partner for you. He presented himself as capable of providing what you needed, supporting you in the way you wanted, taking care of your financial situation, and generally making you happy and satisfied. This is where the control actually began. He was manipulating your first impressions of him in such a way that you believed you had met the perfect partner for you.

In such a circumstance, it was an easy call for you to commit to a relationship with him and plan a future.

However, once you made a firm commitment, the control changed. He maintained control over your perceptions of him (he is marvelous, smart, loving, and successful), and he added direct control over your actions, thoughts, and emotions.

Not only could he make you feel incredibly good, but he could also make you feel incredibly bad. Criticism, humiliation, breaking promises, and outright lying to you all became part of his repertoire.

Your opinions were challenged. You were made to feel bad about your ideas or beliefs. Your thinking evolved to be more in line with his over time. Even if you didn't agree with some of the decisions, you went along with them to keep the peace.

Although you probably didn't realize it at the time, there was a system of rewards and punishments in place. If you got in his way, there was hell to pay. This was the punishment aspect. This was the punishment aspect. If you worked really hard at making life comfortable for him and going along with him, there were rewards of some sort. They may have been few and far between, but there would have been just enough great times to keep you in the relationship, giving you just enough hope during all the upset and misery that things would turn great again. Sometimes the reward was that he didn't yell at you all day.

As a result, your behaviors shifted toward focusing more on him and less on what you wanted. Your entire existence revolved around not upsetting him. He became your life's purpose. Your decisions were based on your assumptions about what he would or would not want, and what would or would not please him.

And if there are children, he most likely has control over them through you. He made the rules, and you had to make sure the kids followed them. He also mistreated the children, lying to them, shouting at them, saying horrible things to them, and even criticizing and blaming you for problems in front of them. In such a situation, a mother's natural reaction is to try to be extra nice to the children in order to compensate for the heinous treatment doled out by him.

Using physical violence once or twice early in the relationship is fairly common with a controlling husband. After that, there may be no more physical abuse, but the threat remains, either spoken or unspoken. This threat is an extremely effective control mechanism. Of course, in some cases, a controlling husband is simply physically abusive on a consistent basis.

Personality Disorders

Many controlling husbands has a personality disorder. This means that their interpersonal relationships are based on exploitation, deception, and coercion. They lack emotions and empathy, which means they are unable to put themselves in the shoes of others; they are not able to feel the pain or distress of those around them. They have a manipulative, callous, impulsive, egocentric, and attention-seeking personality.

The more common name for these types is sociopaths, psychopath and narcissist. If you haven't realized it yet, it can be shocking because most people have a preconceived notion of what a psychopath or narcissist is, and their husband does not fit that description. So let us investigate further.

A Psychopath as a Controlling Husband

A psychopath lacks conscience and has a huge ego. The lack of conscience stems from the absence of emotions, no guilt, remorse, fear, love, embarrassment, empathy or regret. They can do whatever they want and not feel bad about it. This is very important. They can do whatever they want and not feel guilty about it. This clarifies how a psychopathic serial killer can do what he or she does while remaining unaffected by what has happened. However, not all psychopaths are serial killers, and not all serial killers are psychopaths. A very small percentage are serial killers or serial rapists. The vast majority are in society and go unnoticed because they behave like normal humans. They marry, get jobs, and buy houses, and from a distance, they appear to be normal people. In public, they can be charming and friendly.

But, as you are well aware, they can be tyrants and dictators behind closed doors. Because they lack empathy, they can be callous, cruel, abusive, and literally destroy people without feeling bad about it. It can be difficult to accept at first that there are people who do not have emotions. You may even be convinced that your domineering husband does, but there have been numerous instances when your controlling spouse displayed an unusual lack of emotion. For example, no tears at the death of a parent or a complete lack of reaction to the birth of a child.

One emotion your controlling husband will often have is a fierce temper. But even that is odd. He loses his temper for the smallest of reasons or for no reason at all. It can be unpredictable; one day something really irritates him, and the next it's no big deal. And the temper will simply disappear as quickly as it appeared. When he loses it, everyone around him is jolted, and the aftereffects can last for hours. But he can be enraged one moment and then turn around and act as if nothing unusual has happened. This can be very unsettling in and of itself. The explosive anger he displayed one moment is gone the next, and he acts as cool as a cucumber.

It is usually at this point that he criticizes you for being too emotional and unable to control yourself. So you're abused twice for the same incident: the first for being on the receiving end of his rage, and the second is the criticism for being emotionally upset by his rage (which is actually a healthy, normal response to what he was doing). This kind of rage is very psychopathic or narcissistic.

A Narcissist as a Controlling Husband

A narcissist is similar to a psychopath, with the exception that the narcissist always wants to be the center of attention. They want to be praised, adored, and complimented by those around them. This is known as narcissistic supply.

I compare a narcissist to a psychopath (or sociopath) because they both lack conscience and use mind control techniques to control and dominate their victims. From this viewpoint, it makes no difference what specific diagnosis your controlling husband has. Besides, making a formal diagnosis necessitates interviews with trained professionals, a review of past records, and so on, which most socialized psychopaths will not agree to. They will not even admit to being psychopaths. They will almost certainly accuse you of being a controlling psychopath! My point is that some people label their controlling husband as a psychopath, while others label him as a sociopath, and still others label him as a narcissist.

The distinction is academic; what matters is what the controlling husband does and says, because studying these specific things is sufficient to undo the damage they cause.

The Effects of a Controlling Husband

So far, we've seen how a controlling husband alters your beliefs, your thinking, your decision-making, and how he manipulates your emotions. Your perception of the world is altered (he is constantly in your head, and everything revolves around him), as is your behavior in the world (you do stuff to please him and to not upset him).

All of this adds up to a significant change in who you are. Your personality is manipulated to become something else. If friends or family have tried to warn you about him and have said that you are different in some way, it is these changes that they are referring to, though they may not have been as explicit as I have been here. In any case, they were well aware of his profound influence on you, and they were not pleased.

This new personality is a false personality, also known as a pseudopersonality. It is imposed on you without your knowledge or consent. The majority of the influence techniques used against you were used without your awareness of the degree of psychological pressure being applied.

You willingly agreed to some of the changes at the beginning of the relationship because that is what people do in new relationships. You make compromises and find common ground in order to please each other. Even so, you were tricked into thinking you were making your own decisions, because your decisions were based on faulty information, through no fault of your own!

This pseudopersonality was imposed on top of your true personality, and it dominates and suppresses it without ever completely destroying it. This concept helps to explain some of the conflicts that arise when you live with someone who is controlling. Your true personality may object to the treatment and wish to leave, but the pseudopersonality has been programmed to be dependent on the manipulator, and because it is dominant the majority of the time, you end up remaining in an abusive relationship for years. The pseudopersonality is programmed to care for the abuser, but the true personality may despise the controlling husband. These conflicting emotions of hating and needing to care for someone can be extremely distressing, and there is no way to resolve the conflict as long as the pseudopersonality is present. In fact, conflicting emotions, or thoughts that contradict feelings, are very common in someone attempting to cope with a controlling person, and it is one of the reasons the victim may believe they are the problem, or that they are going insane because they can't resolve the conflict.

More on the Pseudopersonality

The psychopath or narcissist programs the pseudopersonality to be subservient and obedient, to care for the manipulator, and to prioritize the manipulator's wants and needs first, second, and third. It regards the manipulator as superior and works hard to gain the manipulator's approval. And it does this even when the victim is arguing back and fighting the manipulator, though often the victim won't like to acknowledge this.

The pseudopersonality is also dependent on the manipulator. Often, the victim cannot imagine a future without the manipulator, which explains why some women leave a controlling husband only to return again. What happens is: the pseudopersonality feels so bad without the manipulator that the only way to feel better is to return to the abuser. Even though the person knows it's a bad thing to do (the true personality), the bad feelings of loneliness, helplessness, and emptiness are so strong that they override logical thinking and return to the abuser.

This does not imply that the victim is codependent, has a weak personality, relies on others to make decisions for her, or enjoys the abuse. People who don't understand mind control and simply blame the victim create these ideas.

The pseudopersonality is created through the use of heavy-duty influence techniques that are used repeatedly, often on a daily basis. Over time, beliefs and behavior patterns are strengthened and reinforced. The manipulator purposefully shapes the victim to be a certain way. The manipulator may not think in terms of pseudopersonality, but is purposefully altering beliefs and behaviors. All of this means that the pseudopersonality doesn't disappear on it's own merely because the person leaves the relationship or the mind control environment. It takes time and effort to piece things together so you can understand how the pseudopersonality was created. Understanding the subtleties of mind control techniques lessens their impact on you, and learning about mind control, narcissists, and psychopaths is the only way to completely reverse their effects.

Another critical factor is that if a person has been in an abusive relationship and hasn't undone their pseudopersonality, the next psychopath they encounter will instantly recognize the beliefs and behaviors of submission, recognize that they have an easy target in front of them, and take aim.

The pseudopersonality is also programmed to reveal information about itself because psychopaths need information to better control their victims. The more information they have the more control they have. Someone who has recently left an abusive situation is often eager to talk about their terrible relationship with others. If this new acquaintance offering a sympathetic ear turns out to be a psychopath or a narcissist, the victim ends up giving them all the details they need to pick up where the previous manipulator left off! This may appear unlikely, but it is actually quite common!

A victim may believe they will recognize another controlling man, but not all controlling people are alike. There is no such thing as a stereotypical controlling husband. The next manipulator will learn what patterns you recognize and will avoid them until you are committed to the relationship, at which point you will be neck deep in another abusive situation by the time you notice the signs of a controlling boyfriend.

What to Do About a Controlling Husband

If your controlling husband is a psychopath or narcissist, the situation is very different from one in which the controlling husband has other reasons for being controlling but still is (genuinely!) willing and open to working on themselves and the relationship to improve things between you. A psychopath or narcissist will not change. They see no reason to change because they regard themselves as superior to others, act as if they are always right, and never doubt themselves.

Given that they will not change, you should never give a psychopath the benefit of the doubt; you cannot negotiate with them (you have tried for years and it simply does not work!) You should never underestimate a psychopath, and the best option is to end the relationship.

Even if there are children, or rather, particularly if there are children, getting out is the best option. Children are expected to have a relationship with both parents. People who say this, however, leave out the rest of the sentence. The complete sentence is that children should have a relationship with both parents unless there is physical, psychological, or sexual abuse. Or, in today's language, unless it isn't in the best interests of the children. Abuse is not in anyone's best interests, especially children, who are the most vulnerable and incapable of protecting themselves.

So get out and get help, because you're going to need it. Help from friends and family, as well as professional help. Working with an expert in this field is well worth it. You've been programmed to believe that you should be able to handle everything on your own, but getting away from a controlling husband is a big deal, and you should accept any help you can get.

An expert will hasten your recovery by helping you in avoiding common mistakes and pitfalls and pointing out things that you may overlook. Speaking about what happened to somebody who doesn't judge or criticize you, understands what you've been through, and can clarify why things happened the way they did is an essential part of your recovery.

Printed in Great Britain
by Amazon

33840440R00020

Captain John Franklin's Lost Expedition: Th
Explorer's Arctic Voyage in Search of the

By Charles River Editors

A painting of the Arctic Council planning a search for Franklin's lost expedition

About Charles River Editors

Charles River Editors is a boutique digital publishing company, specializing in bringing history back to life with educational and engaging books on a wide range of topics. Keep up to date with our new and free offerings with this 5 second sign up on our weekly mailing list, and visit Our Kindle Author Page to see other recently published Kindle titles.

We make these books for you and always want to know our readers' opinions, so we encourage you to leave reviews and look forward to publishing new and exciting titles each week.

Introduction

Stephen C. Dixon's picture of the memorial to the expedition in the Chapel of the Naval College at Greenwich

Captain Franklin's Lost Expedition

Most anyone who has received a basic education in world history knows the story of how "in 1492, Columbus sailed the ocean blue." Most also know that Christopher Columbus made first contact with the Americas while searching for a water route to Asia. However, far fewer people remember that the search for such a route continued for centuries after Columbus' death.

After the discovery of the Americas, several European countries were interested in finding the route, and nations from France to Spain sent out explorers searching for the mysterious route. While these voyages did not reveal the hoped for route, they did result in large parts of both North and South America being mapped, and as more of the new land mass was determined, the parameters of the search for such a route were narrowed. By the 18th century, explorers began to seek such a route to the north, looking for the legendary Northwest Passage.

Eventually, some countries lost interest, but England remained determined, and the masters of the waves continued to send ship after ship and crew after crew across the Atlantic. By the early 19th century, the search was taking expeditions to the Arctic, and each time a team returned to England telling stories of how it was stymied by ice or bad weather, another team confidently went out, certain that it would be the one to make it through.

This ultimately led to the voyage of Sir John Franklin, who left Britain in 1845 for the Arctic in the hopes of completing mapping the Northwest Passage. Instead of returning with spices and silks, Franklin and his men disappeared, leaving behind them a mystery that plagued the English conscience for decades. Ironically, the ill-fated trip only became more legendary when its mystery was solved than it was when it remained a curiosity. It was a tale of ice and cold, starvation and desperation, and a tragically fatal one.

Captain John Franklin's Lost Expedition: The History of the British Explorer's Arctic Voyage in Search of the Northwest Passage chronicles one of the most famous voyages of the 19th century. Along with pictures of important people, places, and events, you will learn about the lost expedition like never before.

Captain John Franklin's Lost Expedition: The History of the British Explorer's Arctic Voyage in Search of the Northwest Passage

About Charles River Editors

Introduction

Free Books by Charles River Editors

Discounted Books by Charles River Editors

Chapter 1: Gospels on Demand

On September 3, 1859, the popular London periodical *The Living Age*, ran a typically Victorian article on the loss of a British hero. Drawing from several recently discovered letters written by a young officer named James Fitzjames, it began, "The sad story takes us back to the June of eighteen hundred and forty-five. The two discovery ships, the Erebus and Terror, are at sea, with the transport containing their supplies in attendance on them. The time is noon; the place on the ocean is near the island of Rona, seventy or eighty miles from Stromness; and the two steamers, Rattler and Blazer, are taking leave — a last, long leave — of the Arctic voyagers. 'Their captains,' says the journal, referring to the two steamers, 'came on board and took our letters; one from me will have told you of our doings up to that time. There was a heavy swell and wind from north-west; but it began veering to west and south-west, which is fair. The steamers then ranged alongside of us, one on each side, as close as possible without touching.... Having done the same to the Terror, away they went, and in an hour or two were out of sight, leaving us with an old gull or two and the rocky Rona to look at; and then was the time to see if any one flinched from the under taking. Every one's cry was, 'Now we are off at last!' No lingering look was cast behind. We drank Lady Franklin's health at the old gentleman's table, and, it being his daughter's birthday, hers too. But the wind, which had become fair as the steamers left (as if to give the latest best news of us), in the evening became foul from the north-west, and we were going northward instead of westward. The sky was clear, the air bracing and exhilarating. I had a slight attack of aguish headache the evening before, but am now clear-headed, and I went to bed thinking of you and dear William, whose portrait is now looking at me.'"

Lady Franklin

Obviously, at the time the writer had no idea he was sailing to his death as part of yet another attempt by a European vessel to find a short cut to Asia. At the time, the *United Service Gazette* observed of Captain John Franklin, "No officer is more suited to such an undertaking, or better acquainted with the locality."

Captain Franklin

Franklin was given two ships for his historic voyage, HMS *Erebus* and HMS *Terror*. Both had been sailed by James Clark Ross, another well-known explorer, to the Arctic in the past and were considered good cold water ships, sturdily built with reinforced bows for cutting through ice and iron rudders that could be pulled into heavy iron wells if the situation necessitated it. Every surface of the ship that could be reinforced had been thus shored up. The ships' most prominent features, however, were their brand new, state of the art propellers. Shaped like screws instead of the traditional bent clover style, they were powered by steam engines formerly used to power locomotives. The ships also featured steam heating and a library of over 1,000 books.

A painting depicting the *Erebus* and *Terror*

James Clark Ross

Franklin was particularly proud of the rations he carried on board; his crew would not be forced to live on salt pork and dried beans, nor would they be driven by starvation to gouge small plants out of frozen tundra to survive. Ironically, before the expedition he proudly declared that the 30,000 pounds of canned meat and vegetables, sealed in tin cans by the latest technology, would ensure the crewmembers "will never starve again. It will nourish us through winter, spring, and summer."

This was understandably important to the man who had once written of an earlier incident, "A small quantity of tripe de roche [a type of lichen] was gathered; and Credit, who had been hunting, brought in the antlers and back bone of a deer which had been killed in the summer. The wolves and birds of prey had picked them clean, but there still remained a quantity of the spinal marrow which they had not been able to extract. This, although putrid, was esteemed a valuable prize, and the spine being divided into portions, was distributed equally. After eating the marrow, which was so acrid as to excoriate the lips, we rendered the bones friable by burning, and ate them also."

In fact, Franklin's tale of another incident of near starvation had earned him a notorious nickname: "The Man Who Ate His Boots."

Chapter 2: The Beginning of the Voyage

The ships sailed from England on May 19, 1845, the 59 year-old Franklin having kissed his wife, Lady Jane, goodbye, and traveled along the coast, putting into port one last time before striking out across the Atlantic. *The Morning Herald* reported on June 14, "The screw-propeller steam-sloop Rattler, Commander G. W. Smith, commanding pro ten., arrived at Sheerness on Monday, at 11h. 30m. o'clock from the Orkney Islands, after having towed the Erebus, Captain Sir John Franklin, and the Terror, Captain Crozier, to Cape Wrath, and thence to the islands Barra and Rona, situated 60 miles N.W. of the Orkneys, where the ships composing the Arctic expedition took their final departure about noon, on the 4th instant, under the auspices of as favourable a breeze as could be well desired to waft them towards the icy region they have been sent to explore."

The *Herald* also reported the tremendous enthusiasm these voyages elicited, which made sense since these explorers were the pioneers of their generation, breaking previous boundaries to go where nobody else had gone before. "At parting a most exhilarating scene occurred, which will doubtlessly remain in the memory of all that had the gratification of participating in the farewell cheer to the brave fellows that have volunteered in so laudable and perilous a service. At this time the Erebus and Terror, and Baretto Junior, transport, were hove to, rolling heavily from the violent swell that the recent gales had produced; a signal flying from the masthead of the Erebus indicated Sir John Franklin's order for all captains to proceed on board to receive their final instructions; this order having been completed, their return to their respective ships was the time chosen for manning the rigging of the two steamers in attendance. At the sound of the boatswain's pipe, the shrouds of the Rattler and Blazer were in one instant lined by their crews, all anxious to outvie each other in the pleasing task they were about to perform. The word was given and three cheers, loud and hearty as ever escaped the lungs of British tars, saluted the ears of Sir John Franklin and his gallant colleagues; in turn the crews of the discovery ships manned their rigging, and, with their respective commanders and officers on the quarter-deck, gave vent to cheers so long and powerful as to leave not the slightest doubt of the physical energies of the men they came from, and their consequent fitness to encounter the difficulties that may shortly surround them…"

Leading the expedition with Franklin were several veterans of similar voyages. The crew included Francis Rawdon Moira Crozier, an experienced officer who might have been given command of the expedition had his family connections been grander. James Fitzjames was considered by many to be as capable as Franklin, though significantly younger. He was sent along to captain the *Eremus*, while Crozier commanded the *Terror*. Sailing with these men were about 130 others, sailors and officers alike. It was the largest expedition of its kind up to that time in history, and though every man knew their goal was to sail through the Northwest Passage to the Pacific, no one could have known the coming cost.

Crozier

At the last minute, some of the crew chose to leave the ships and visit family members while the ships were stopped in Scotland. For his part, Fitzjames did not begrudge them their decisions, writing, "Our men are all fine, hearty fellows, mostly north-countrymen, with a few men-of-war's men. We feared at Stromness that some of them would repent, and it is usual to allow no leave — the 1 error did not. But two men wanted to see — one his wife, whom he had not seen for four years, and the other his mother, whom he had not seen for seventeen — so I let them go to Kirkwall, fourteen miles off. I also allowed a man of each mess to go on shore for provisions."

This, unfortunately, led to problems, as he noted: "They all came on board to their leave; but finding we were not going to sea till the following morning, four men (who probably had taken a leetle too much whiskey, among them was the little old man who had not seen his wife for four years) took a small boat that lay alongside, and went on shore without leave. Their absence was soon discovered, and Fairholme, assisted by Baillie, and somebody or other, brought all on board by three o'clock in the morning. I firmly believe each intended coming on board (if he had been sober enough), especially the poor man with the wife; but, according to the rules of the service, these men should have been severely punished — one method being to stop their pay and give it to the constables, or others, who apprehended them. It struck me, however, that the punishment is intended to prevent misconduct in others, and not to revenge their individual misconduct: men know very well when they are in the wrong, and there is clearly no chance of any repetition of the offence until we get to Valparaiso, or the Sandwich Islands; so I got up at four o'clock, had everybody on deck, sent Gore and the sergeant of marines below, and searched the whole deck for spirits, which were thrown overboard. This took two good hours, soon after which we up anchor, and made sail out. I said nothing to any of them. They evidently expected a rowing, and the old man with the wife looked very sheepish, and would not look me in the face; but nothing more was said, and the men have behaved not a bit the worse ever since."

The trans-Atlantic crossing itself was uneventful, with various entries in Fitzjames' journal telling stories of the sea being "a beautiful, delicate, cold-looking green" with waves like "long rollers, as if carved out of the essence of glass bottles." Based on what Fitzjames recorded, *The Living Age* filled in other details: "The rate of sailing is so rapid, with the high wind in their favor, that they get within six miles of Ice land. On the 14th [of June] the rain pours down and the fogs close round them. The Erebus sails on through the dense obscurity, with the Terror on one side, and the transport on the other, all three keeping close together for fear of losing each other. On this day the officers amuse themselves by arranging their books, and find to their satisfaction that they can produce a very sufficient library. Ice-master Reid comes out in his quaint, experienced way with a morsel of useful information on the subject of cookery. He sees the steward towing some fish overboard to try and get a little of the salt out of it; roars out sarcastically, 'What are you making faces at there? That's not the way to get the salt out;' and instructs the steward to boil the fish first, and then to take it off the fire and keep it just not boiling. It is Saturday night when Reid sets matters right with the salt fish; and he and Purser Osmar socially hob- and-nob together, drinking the favorite sea-toast of Sweethearts and Wives, and asking Captain Fitzjames to join them. He, poor fellow, meets them with his light-hearted joke, in return — says he has not got a sweetheart and does not want a wife — and ends the entry in his journal, for that day, by writing ' good night ' to his dear friends in England."

One cannot help but feel glad that the men had some small pleasures in the last happy months of their lives and found time to pursue enjoyable tasks, in addition to their normal work on the ships. *The Living Age* also observed, "On the 18th, they make a catalogue of their little library; and, remembering that it is 'Waterloo Day,' drink the Duke of Wellington's health at Sir John Franklin's table. On this day, also, the 'crow's nest' is completed. It is usually 'a cask lined with canvas, at the fore-topmast head, for a man to stand in to look out for channels in the ice;' on board the Erebus, however, it is 'a sort of canvas cylinder, hooped.' Ice-master Reid is to be perched up in this observatory, and criticises it, with his north-country eye on the main chance, as 'a very expensive one.' At ten at night — the time which, allowing for difference of longitude, answers to half-past seven in London — Captain Fitzjames takes a glass of brandy-and-water, in honor of his own anticipated promotion at the brevet of the 18th, which has been talked of in England. He pleases himself with the idea that he is taking an imaginary glass of wine with Mr. and Mrs. Coningham, at that moment; and, while he is telling them this in the journal, Reid comes in, and sees him writing as usual. 'Why, Mister Jems,' says the surprised ice-master, perplexedly scratching his head, ' you never seem to me to sleep at arl ; you're always writin' !'"

Though the quarters were cramped, the men seemed to have gotten along well together, at least according to Fitzjames. "In our mess we have the following, whom I shall probably from time to time give you descriptions of: First Lieutenant, Gore; second, Le Vescomte; third, Fairholme; purser, Osmar; surgeon, Stanley; assistant- surgeon, Goodsir; ice-master (so-called) Reid; mates — Sargent, Des Voeux, Crouch; second master, Collins; commander, you know better than he does himself. The most original character of all — rough, intelligent, unpolished, with a broad, north country accent, but not vulgar, good-humored, and honest-hearted — is Reid, a Greenland whaler, native of Aberdeen, who has commanded whaling vessels, and amuses us with his quaint remarks and descriptions of the ice, catching whales, etc. For instance, he just said to me, on my saying we should soon be off Cape Farewell at this rate, and asking if one might not generally expect a gale off it (Cape Farewell being the south point of Greenland), 'Ah! now, Mister Jems, we'll be having the weather fine, sir! fine. No ice at arl about it, sir, unless it be the bergs — arl the ice'll be gone, sir, only the bergs, which I like to see. Let it come on to blow, look out for a big 'un. Get under his lee, and hold on to him fast, sir, fast. If he drifts near the land, why, he grounds afore you do.' The idea of all the ice being gone, except the ice bergs, is racy beyond description. I have just had a game of chess with the purser, Osmar, who is delightful. ... I was at first inclined to think he was a stupid old man, because he had a chin and took snuff; but he is as merry- hearted as any young man, full of quaint, dry sayings, always good-humored, always laugh ing, never a bore, takes his pinch after dinner, plays a rubber, and beats me at chess — and, he is a gentleman."

In a manner reminiscent of the hero worship many young men feel for their commander, Fitzjames reserved his highest praise for his captain, writing enthusiastically of their early encounters: "6th June. — Today Sir John Franklin showed me such part of his instructions as related to the main purpose of our voyage, and the necessity of observing everything from a flea to a whale in the unknown regions we are to visit. He also told me I was especially charged with the magnetic observations. He then told all the officers that he was desired to claim all their remarks, journals, sketches, etc., on our return to England, and read us some parts of his instructions to the officers of the Trent, the first vessel he commanded, in 1818, with Captain Buchan, on an attempt to reach the North Pole, pointing out how desirable it is to note everything, and give one's individual opinion on it. He spoke delightfully of the zealous co-operation he expected from all, and his desire to do full justice to the exertions of each. ... At dinner, today, Sir John gave us a pleasant account of his expectations of being able to get through the ice on the coast of America, and his disbelief in the idea that there is open sea to the northward. He also said he believed it to be possible to reach the Pole over the ice by wintering at Spitzbergen, and going in the spring before the ice broke up and drifted to the south, as it did with Parry on it. . . . 8th. — I like a man who is in earnest. Sir John Franklin read the Church-service today and a sermon so very beautifully, that I defy any man not to feel the force of what he would convey. The first Sunday he read was a day or two before we sailed, when Lady Franklin, his daughter, and niece attended. Everyone was struck with his extreme earnestness of manner, evidently proceeding from real conviction. . . . We are very fond of Sir John Franklin, who improves very much as we come to know more of him. He is anything but nervous or fidgety; in fact, I should say remarkable for energetic decision in sudden emergencies; but I should think he might be easily persuaded where he has not already formed a strong opinion."

The men sailed on and, according to *The Living Age*, "On the 21st the ships are in Davis' Straits; bottle-nose whales are plunging and tumbling all round them; and tree-trunks, with the bark rubbed off by the ice, are floating by. The next day is Sunday: it is blowing hard, and the ships are rolling prodigiously; but they contrive to struggle through the Church service on the lower deck. The 23d brings a downright gale; the dinner party in Sir John's cabin has to be given up, the host finding that his guests cannot combine the two actions of holding on and eating and drinking at the same time. The next day is calmer; and the Arctic cold begins to make itself so sensibly felt, that the ship's monkey is obliged to be clothed in a blanket, frock, and trousers, which the sailors have made for her. On the 25th, they sight the coast of Greenland, 'rugged and sparkling with snow.' The sea is now of a delicate blue in the shadows, and so calm that 'the Terror's mast-heads are reflected close alongside, though she is half a mile off. The air is delightfully cool and bracing, and everybody is in good-humor either with himself or his neighbors. Captain Fitzjames has been on deck all day, taking observations. Goodsir is catching the most extraordinary animals in a net, and is in ecstacies. Gore and Des Voeux are over the side, poking with nets and long poles, with cigars in their mouths, and Osmar laughing."

For all that their voyage was a pleasant one, the men were grateful when they finally began to draw near land. *The Living Age* explained, "The 1st of July brings the ships within a day's sail of Whale-fish Islands at which place the transport is to be unloaded of her provisions and coals, and left to return to England. On the evening of that day, there are sixty-five icebergs in sight; and the vessels sail in "among a shoal of some hundred walruses, tumbling over one another, diving and splashing with their fins and tails, and looking at the ships with their grim, solemn-looking countenances and small heads, bewhiskered and betusked." On the 2d, they find themselves in a fog, "right under a dense, black-looking coast topped with snow." This is Disco, a Danish settlement. The scenery is grand, but desolate beyond expression. At midnight, Captain Fitzjames finds Purser Osmar on deck, cheerfully dancing with an imaginary skipping-rope. "What a happy fellow you are," says Captain Fitzjames; "always in good humor." "Well, sir," answers cheerful Osmar, "If I am not happy here, I don't know where else I could be." The 4th finds them safe in their temporary haven at the Whalefish Islands. The next day, every man is on shore, "running about for a sort of holiday, getting eider ducks' eggs, curious mosses and plants, and shells." It is warm enough again, now, for the mosquitoes to be biting."

Of course, there was more to do than just gather unique specimens. *The Living Age* speculated, "During this fine weather, the transport will probably be un loaded, either on Monday the 7th, or Tuesday the 8th; and on the 9th or 10th, the two Discovery Ships will perhaps be on their way to Lancaster Sound. It is reported that this is the mildest and earliest summer known in those regions, and that the ice is clear all the way through the coming voyage. Guided by Sir John Franklin's experience, the officers expect to reach Lancaster Sound as soon as the 1st of August; but this information is not to be generally communicated in England from the fear of making the public too sanguine about the season. Captain Fitzjames' own idea is that they have 'a good chance of getting through this year, if it is to be done at all; 'but he is himself privately inclined to hope that no such extraordinary luck may happen to them, as he wants 'to have a winter for magnetic observations.' With this little outhreak of professional enthusiasm, and with this description of the future prospects of the expedition, the deeply interesting narrative draws to a close."

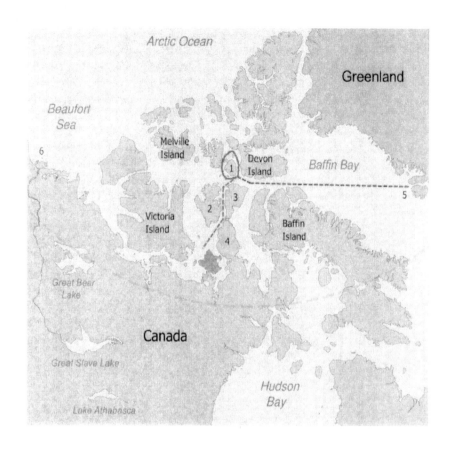

Arctic Ocean

Greenland

Beaufort
Sea

6

Melville
Island

Devon
Island

Baffin Bay

1

3

5

Victoria
Island

2

Baffin
Island

4

Great Bear
Lake

Canada

Great Slave Lake

Hudson
Bay

Lake Athabasca

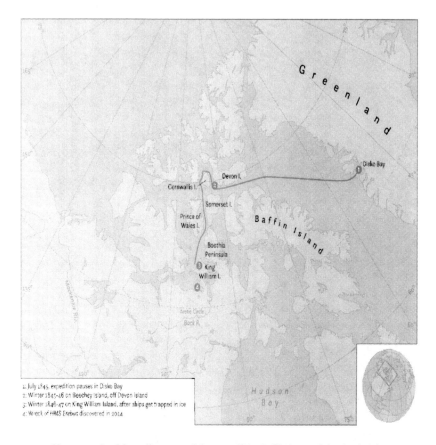

Hans van der Maarel's maps of the expedition's likely route in the Arctic

1: July 1845, expedition pauses in Disko Bay
2: Winter 1845-46 on Beechey Island, off Devon Island
3: Winter 1846-47 on King William Island, after ships get trapped in ice
4: Wreck of HMS Erebus discovered in 2014

The group arrived in Greenland in late June 1845, took on supplies, and dispatched some letters back to England, along with five men who were fortunate enough to decide to return home at this point. Not surprisingly, some of the letters were, at least to a certain extent, propaganda meant to cast the trip in a favorable light, and they were duly published. "We have been favoured with the sight of letters from Mr. H. Goodsir, who is attached to this expedition, and hasten to communicate to our readers an outline of the results already obtained. The zeal and scientific knowledge of our friend Mr. Goodsir have raised high anticipations of the value to natural science of this voyage, and these have, if possible, attained a still greater elevation by what has been already done. It is most satisfactory to learn that the officers of the expedition, and also a considerable number of the men, are most active in rendering every assistance to him in his researches. They have indeed kept him at work almost night and day (if there can be said to be any night in these latitudes), examining, drawing, and describing new or highly interesting animals."

The first letter was dated July 7, 1845 and read, "The earlier part of the voyage was rather tedious, owing to adverse and stormy winds, so that the ships were driven far to the north-east, near enough on June 11th to have seen the mountains of Iceland, had the state of the atmosphere allowed. On the 22nd they were off Cape Farewell, the southern point of Greenland. Up to this date there were only two days upon which he could make any observations, but the results of these are extremely interesting. On the 10th of June, in lat. 61° 47; , long. 14° 14; , numerous specimens of a species of Briareus were obtained, furnishing an important addition to our knowledge of these animals. ... On the 23rd of June, having rounded Cape Farewell in a heavy gale of wind on the preceding day, on entering Davis' Straits numerous beautiful Pteropoda of the genus Clio were obtained in company with Spiratella. They were swimming actively in the water and were adorned with the brightest colours; only approaching the surface of the sea on calm evenings. ... Mr. Goodsir is making minute observations upon the ice of the bergs, and as he purposes continuing them throughout the voyage, there can be little doubt of his arriving at valuable conclusions. He observes that it is quite without salt; this was to be expected, when we consider that they are not formed of marine ice, but are parts of glaciers which have become detached and fallen into the sea."

The article concluded, "The expedition has now proceeded into the inhospitable icy regions of the north, and we must not expect to receive any further accounts of it until it has either succeeded in making its way into the Pacific Ocean, or having found that to be impossible, is on its return to England. In either case there can be no doubt that much valuable scientific information will be obtained."

As far as Goodsir was concerned, the voyage was a chance of a lifetime to make new scientific discoveries, even if the more military-minded men on board found him to be something of an unusual species himself. Fitzjames said of him, "6th, towards midnight. — I can't make out why Scotchmen just caught always speak in a low, hesitating, monotonous tone of voice, which is not at all times to be understood; this is, I believe, called 'cannyness.' Mr. Goodsir is ' canny.' He is long and straight, and walks upright on his toes, with his hands tucked up in each jacket pocket. He is perfectly good-humored, very well informed on general points, in natural history learned, was Curator of the Edinburgh Museum, appears to be about twenty-eight years of age, laughs delightfully, cannot be in a passion, is enthusiastic about all 'ologies, draws the insides of microscopic animals with an imaginary pointed pencil, catches phenomena in a bucket, looks at the thermometer and every other meter, is a pleasant companion, and an acquisition to the mess…"

Goodsir

Even with the hindsight of knowing how the voyage ended, *The Living Age* painted a very pleasant picture indeed for its readers, waxing lyrical as it talked of the men sailing on through the cold: "They are very happy. How delightfully the little strokes of character in the journal open the view to us of the cheerful, simple-hearted, social intercourse of the sailor-brotherhood! How vividly, between tears and smiles, we see the honest faces round the mess-table, as day by day draws the good ship nearer and nearer to the cruel north! Purser Osmar, taking his after-dinner pinch, and playing his rubber; long, straight, pleasantly-laughing Goodsir, matching his learning and his science against ice-master Reid, and his natural north-country sharpness; plump, white-handed Surgeon Stanley, with an attentive eye to the appointments of the mess-table; little, quiet, steady, black-haired Crouch, listening to the conversation, while sweet-tempered DesVoeux keeps it going pleasantly, and Graham Gore sits near at hand, ready to while away the time, when the talk flags, with a tune on his flute; — one by one, these members of the doomed ship's company appear before us again; fold by fold, the snowy veil wreathed over them is melted from view, and the dead and gone come back to us for a little while from the icy keeping of Death."

Chapter 3: Initial Searches for the Crew

The last visual contact made with the expedition occurred on July 28, 1845, when the group passed a whaling ship. At that time, all appeared to be well. However, after a year had passed with no word of any sightings of the expedition, it was clear that all was not well. Lady Franklin began lobbying Parliament to send out a search part for her husband and his men. As is too often the case, the government dragged its feet, insisting that there was nothing to be concerned about. Then, another year passed, and another, and the public, fascinated by the expedition and its seeming disappearance, began to ask questions about its progress and demand that the crewmembers be found.

In 1850, the Reverend William Scoresby wrote in his book, *The Franklin expedition: or, Considerations on measures for the discovery and relief of our absent adventurers in the Arctic regions*, "In the year 1848, researches in three different quarters, and by three separate expeditions, were appointed to be undertaken by the Government. By Behring Strait, the Plover, Commander Moore, was ordered on the search; whilst Captain Kellett, of the Herald, surveying-vessel, then in the Pacific, was instructed to take the Plover under his direction, for joint research after, and relief of, the expedition under Sir John Franklin. The Plover left England on the 31st of January, 1848, but, being a wretched sailer, made such slow progress that she did not reach Woahoo, in the Sandwich Islands, until the 22d of August — a period of the year too late for any effective operations within the Arctic circle. The Herald, meanwhile, went northward as far as Cape Krusenstern, Kotzebue Sound, which she left for the southward — not being prepared to winter, nor for explorations among ice — on the 29th of September. The Plover was not met with during this progress of the Herald, nor any tidings heard of the missing expedition of Sir John Franklin."

Another group was soon dispatched, and Scoresby continued, "The second division, for search, was the overland and boat expedition, under Sir John Richardson, for the exploration of the Arctic Sea betwixt the Mackenzie and Coppermine Rivers, east and west: and intermediate between the northern coast of the American continent, and lands lying proximate thereto, north and south: — it being supposed that, if Sir John Franklin's party had been compelled to abandon their ships and take to their boats, they might very probably make for this coast. ... The Commander of the expedition, accompanied by Dr. Rae, left Liverpool on the 25th of March, 1848.... In this enterprise, the coast line from the Mackenzie to the Coppermine, was, according to Sir John Richardson's instructions, carefully examined: whilst several hundreds of Es[kimoes] (comprising numerous parties and various tribes) were communicated with in respect of the object of their search, but without any trace of the missing expedition being met with, or any tidings of it being obtained. ... Sir John Richardson, after wintering at Fort Confidence, commenced, along with the Europeans and some others of the party, their return homeward. in the beginning of May, and arrived in England on the 6th of November, 1849, —having left Dr. Rae, with a small but effective party, who volunteered for the service, to make the unaccomplished researches during the summer of that year."

There was one more party sent out and, according to Scoresby, they very nearly shared Franklin's fate. "The third, and most expensively appointed, section of the expeditions for search, was that under Sir James Ross and Captain Burd— comprising two ships, the Enterprize and Investigator. These left the Thames on the 12th of May, 1848; entered Basin Bay early in July; left the Danish settlement of Upemavik on the 13th of that month; cleared the Middle Ice, August the 20th, and entered the harbour of Port Leopold, where they wintered (and, it may be added, summered too) on the 11th of September. During the months of May and June, 1849, the north and west coasts of North Somerset were explored, and some other journeys, of little importance, made. It was not till August the 28th, that the ships succeeded in getting clear of their harbour — having been there detained for a year, lacking only a fortnight! On the 1st of September — the fourth day after their release — the ships got unfortunately beset in a pack of floating ice, where, helplessly detained, they were drifted along with it fairly out of Lancaster Sound into Baffin Bay, and did not obtain their release till the 24th or 25th of September, — a period deemed too late to attempt any further enterprises in these frigid regions. On the 3rd of November they arrived off Scarborough."

Another ship was in fact lost while looking for Franklin's expedition. Scoresby admitted, "Finally, we have to notice, the sending out of the North Star, store-ship, Mr. James Saunders, master commanding, into Baffin Bay, in the summer of 1849.... The North Star sailed from the Thames on the 16th May, 1849, and was seen July 19th...waiting for a passage round, or through, the Middle Ice of Baffin Bay, and has not since been heard of."

Ultimately, it was Dr. John Rae who returned to the Arctic years later and uncovered information that was both revealing and revolting. In 1854, he made contact with an Inuit tribe that happened to have a number of items connected with the expedition. He recorded an important encounter in his journal, "This man was very communicative, and on putting to him the usual questions as to his having seen "white men' before, or any ships or boats, he replied in the negative; but said that a party of 'Kabloonans' had died of starvation a long distance to the west of where we then were, and beyond a large river. He stated that he did not know the exact place, that he never had been-there and that he could not accompany us so far."

Rae

Rae later reported the following to the Secretary of the Admiralty: "I have the honour to mention, for the information of my Lords Commissioners of the Admiralty, that during my journey over the ice and snow this spring, with the view of completing the survey of the west shore of Boothia, I met with Esquimanx in Felly Bay, from one of whom I learned that a party of white men (Kablonnans) had perished from want of food some distance to the westward, and not far beyond a large river, containing many falls and rapids. Subsequently, farther particulars were received, and a number of articles purchased, which places the fate of a portion, if not of all, of the then survivors of Sir John Franklin's long-lost party beyond a doubt—a fate as terrible as the imagination can conceive. The substance of the information obtained at various times and from various sources was as follows: In the spring, four winters past (spring, 1850), a party of 'white men,' amounting to about 40, were seen travelling southward over the ice and dragging a boat with them by some Esquimaux, who were killing seals near the north shore of King William's Land; which is a large island. None of the party could speak the Esquimaux language intelligibly, but by signs the natives were made to understand that their ship, or ships, had been crushed by ice, and that they were now going to where they expected to find deer to shoot. From the appearance of the men, all of whom, except one officer, looked thin, they were then supposed to be getting short of provisions, and purchased a small seal from the natives."

Having been spared, at least temporarily, from death, the party continued on, but apparently not for long. Rae continued, "At a later date the same season, but previous to the breaking up of the ice, the bodies of some 30 persons were discovered on the Continent, and five on an island near it, about a long day's journey to the N. W. of a large stream, which can be no other than Back's Great Fish River (named by the Esquimaux Doot-ko-hi-calik) as its description, and that of the low shore in the neighbourhood of Point Ogle and Montreal Island agree exactly with that of Sir George Back. Some of the bodies had been buried (probably those of the first victims of famine), some were in a tent or tents, others under the boat which had been turned over to form a shelter, and several lay scattered about in different directions. Of those found on the island one was supposed to have been an officer, as he bad a telescope strapped over his shoulders, and his double- barreled gun lay underneath him. From the mutilated state of many of the corpses and the contents of the kettles, it is evident that our wretched countrymen had been driven to the last resource—cannibalism—as a means of prolonging existence."

After this shocking revelation, Rae, perhaps knowing that his readers would be reluctant to accept his report, added more details: "There appeared to have been an abundant stock of ammunition, as the powder was emptied in a heap on the ground by the natives out of the kegs or cases containing it; and a quantity of ball and shot was found below high water mark, having probably been left on the ice close to the beach. There must have been a number of watches, compasses, telescopes, guns (several double-barrelled) &c., all of which appear to have been broken up, as I saw pieces of those different articles with the Esquimaux, together with some silver spoons and forks. I purchased as many as I could get. A list of the most important of these I enclose, with a rough sketch of the crests and initials of the forks and spoons. The articles themselves shall be handed over to the Secretary of the Hudson's Bay Company on my arrival in London. None of the Esquimaux with whom I conversed had seen the 'whites,' nor had they ever been at the place where the bodies were found; but had their information from those who had been there, and who had seen the party when travelling."

Though he did not mention it in his report, Rae seemed to think that a few men survived the winter, confiding in his journal, "A few of the unfortunate men must have survived until the arrival of the wildfowl (say until the end of May), as shot were heard and fresh bones and feathers of geese were noticed near the scene of the sad event."

One wonders what happened to these men. Did they die later that winter? Were they overcome by shame eating their dead comrades? Did they decide to disappear into the Arctic territory? There is no way to know for sure, and Rae did not even try to speculate. He did, however, list the items he had obtained that had obviously once belonged to the lost party. They included the following:

"1 silver table fork—crest, an animal's head with wing, extended above

3 silver table forks—crest, a bird with wings extended

1 silver table spoon—crest, with initials F. R. M. C. (Captain Crozier, Terror)

1 silver table spoon and 1 fork—crest, bird with laurel branch in month motto, 'Spero tneliora'

1 silver table spoon, 1 tea spoon, and 1 dessert fork—crest, a fish's head looking upwards, with laurel branches on each side

1 silver table fork—initials, 'H. D. S. G.' (Harry D. S. Goodsir, assistant-Burgeon, Erebus)

1 silver table fork—initials, 'A. M'D.' (Alexander McDonald, assistant-surgeon, Terror)

1 silver table fork—initials, 'G. A. M.' (Gillies A. Macbean, second-master, Terror)

1 silver table fork—initials, 'J. T.'

1 silver dessert spoon—initials, 'J. S.P.' (John S. Peddie, surgeon, Erebus)

1 round silver plate, engraved, 'Sir John Franklin, K.C.B.'

A star or order, with motto, 'Nec aspera terrent, G.R.III., MDCCOXV.'

Also a number of other articles with no marks by which they could be recognised, but which will be handed over with those above named to the Secretary of the Hon. Hudson's Bay Company."

Not surprisingly, the British government refused to believe that their best and brightest had become cannibals. Instead, officials maintained that the party had simply become lost and died in the frozen hell they had gone into. Decades later, skeletal remains found at various places along their path would tell the sad tale of how the men first took the time and energy to bury their dead, only to finally give up on the effort and allow the bodies to lie where they fell. Some Inuits later claimed that they had cared for four white men during the winter of 1851 and had seen them off on their journey that spring, a full 6 years after the launching of the voyage, but if so, those men were never heard from again.

Chapter 4: Filling In More Blanks

Various expeditions continued to set out from England from time to time in search of the lost expedition and, while some were no doubt humanitarian in nature, many of the men were after the substantial reward being offered, as Scoresby noted: "There remains only to be noticed, in connection with these records of the results of the means for search hitherto put into operation, the rewards which have been offered, for the stimulating of private, as well as public, enterprise in this cause of humanity. The devoted and persevering wife of the commander of the missing expedition, was the first to endeavour, by her private means, to stimulate research on the part of the whalers, by offering, in 1848, a reward of £2000, and in 1849, one of £3000, "or a proportion thereof according to services rendered, to any ship or ships, which, departing from the usual fishing grounds, might discover, and, if needed, afford effectual relief to the missing expedition, or any portion of it." ... By Her Majesty's Government, another pecuniary reward, £20,000, was offered in March, 1849, with the view of a further stimulation of enterprise. This sum was assured " to such private ship, or by distribution among such private ships, or to any exploring party or parties, of any country, as might, in the judgment of the Board of Admiralty, have rendered efficient assistance to Sir John Franklin, his ships, or their crews, and might have contributed directly to extricate them from the ice.'"

Lady Franklin sent out some of the parties by using her own money, and among the parties she sent out was one led by Sir Francis Leopold McClintock. In 1858, he and his men landed on King William Island, where he found an abandoned boat mounted on a sled and loaded with worn equipment and two skeletons. He also located a metal can containing one sheet of paper giving a detailed report of what had happened to the crew. *The Stratford Times* reported in October 1859, "[A]t last the mystery of Franklin's fate is solved. We know (says the Times) where he died—the very day of his death. More than twelve years ago the ardent spirit of John Franklin passed away amid a world of ice and snow. And, indeed, it would seem that the trials of his previous explorations, and the anxieties attendant upon the beginning of his last search for the North-West Passage, had proved too much for his iron frame before the calamities and disasters for which Captain McClintock has prepared us came upon the rest of the expedition. ...he died surrounded by comrades and friends, and in the discharge of his duty. No soldier or sailor can desire or hope a nobler fate. The condolences and sympathies of a nation accompany the sorrows of his widow and the griefs of his friends, but it is not altogether out of place for the country to express its satisfaction that the lives of brave sailors were not uselessly sacrificed in a series of expeditions which should have borne for their motto, "Hoping against hope." So far it is satisfactory to know the final search has proved that Sir John Franklin is dead. ... At Point Victory, on the north-west coast of King William's Island, a record of the proceedings of the Franklin Expedition was found, dated April 25, 1848, and signed by Captain Crozier and Captain Fitzjames. The story it told appears to have been simple and sad enough—Sir John Franklin had died nearly ten months before—on the 11th of June, 1847. The expedition seems then to have worked on as well as it could, and, as soon as the ice permitted, to have proceeded with its mission, but month after month of battle with frost and ice, and snow passed away—difficulties no doubt were encountered which none of us who sit at home can realise, and on one fatal day, the 22nd of April, 1848, the Erebus and the Terror were abandoned by their crews, 15 miles N.N.W. of Point Victory. The "survivors," which is a term that indicates other losses than that of the great seaman who led them, to the number of 105, two days after the abandonment of the vessels, reached the island, erected a cairn, concealed the record, and were then about to proceed for the Great Fish River, under the command of Captain Crozier."

McClintock

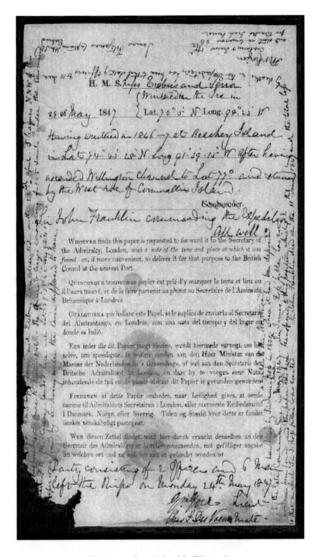

The note found by McClintock

McClintock's journal, portions of which were published in the *Times*, provided further details of the search: "Early spring journeys were commenced on the 17th of February, 1859, by Captain Young and myself. Captain Young carrying his depot across to Prince of Wales' land, while I went southward, towards the magnetic pole, in the hope of communicating with the Esquimaux, and obtaining such information as might lead us at once to the object of our search.

On the 28th of February, when near Cape Victoria, we had the good fortune to meet a small party of natives, and were subsequently visited by about 45 Individuals. For four days we remained in communication with them, obtaining many relics, and the information that several years ago a ship was crushed by the ice off the north shore, of King William's Island, but that all her people landed safely, and went away to the Great Fish River, where they died. This tribe was well supplied with wood, obtained, they said, from a boat left by the white men on the Great River. On the 2nd of April our long projected spring journeys were commenced; Lieutenant Hobson accompanied me as far as Cape Victoria, each of us had a sledge drawn by four men, and an auxiliary sledge drawn by six dogs. This was all the force we could muster."

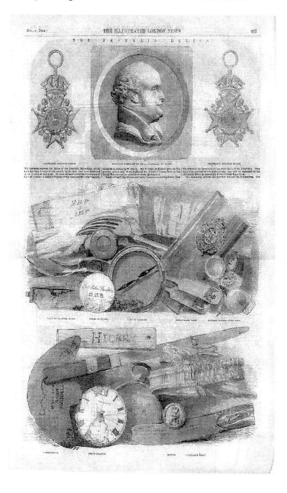

Newspaper depictions of relics collected from the lost expedition

He also jotted down details of how he came into possession of so many items from the expedition: "Accompanied by my own party and Mr. Petersen, I marched along the east shore of King William's Island, occasionally passing deserted snow huts, but without meeting natives till the 8th of May, when off Cape Norton we arrived at a snow village containing about 30 inhabitants. … Many more relics of our countrymen were obtained; we could not carry away all we might have purchased. They pointed to the inlet we had crossed the day before, and told us that one day's march up it, and thence four days overland brought them to the wreck. None of these people had been there since 1857-8, at which time they said but little remained, their countrymen having carried away almost everything. Most of our information was received from an intelligent old woman; she said It was on the fall of the year that the ship was forced ashore;

many of the white men dropped by the way as they went towards the Great River; but this was only known to them in the winter following, when their bodies were discovered."

The next few weeks revealed more and more evidence, much of it gruesome, of what had become of the lost explorers. McClintock explained, "Recrossing the Strait to King William's Island, we continued the examination of its southern shore without success until the 24th of May, when about ten miles eastward of Cape Herschell a bleached skeleton was found, around which lay fragments of European clothing. Upon carefully removing the snow a small pocket-book was found, containing a few letters. These, although much decayed, may yet be deciphered. Judging from the remains of his dress, this unfortunate young man was a steward or officer's servant, and his position exactly verified the Esquimaux's assertion, that they dropped as they walked along. ... After parting from me at Cape Victoria on the 28th of April Lieutenant Hobson made for Cape Felix. At a short distance westward of it he found a very large cairn, and close to it three small tents, with blankets, old clothes, and other relics of a shooting or magnetic station; but although the cairn was dug under, and a trench dug all round it at a distance of 10 feet, no record was discovered. A piece of blank paper folded up was found in the cairn, and two broken bottles, which may, perhaps, have contained records, lay beside it among some stones which had fallen from off the top. The most interesting of the articles discovered here, including a boat's ensign, were brought away by Mr. Hobson. About two miles further to the south-west a small cairn was found, but neither records nor relics obtained. About three miles north of Point Victory a second small cairn was examined, but only a broken pickaxe and empty canister found."

Though discouraged by the lack of information provided by the cairns they had found thus far, the men persevered in their search and were finally rewarded. According to McClintock, "On the 6th of May, Lieutenant Hobson pitched his tent beside a large cairn upon Point Victory. Lying among some loose stones which had fallen from the top of this cairn was found a small tin case containing a record, the substance of which is briefly as follows:— "This cairn was built by the Franklin expedition, upon the assumed site of Sir James Ross's pillar, which had not been found. The Erebus and Terror spent their first winter at Beechey Island, after having ascended Wellington Channel...and returned by the west side of Cornwallis Island. ... Sir J. Franklin died on the 11th of June, 1847. On the 22nd of April, 1848, the ships were abandoned five leagues to the N.N.W. of Point Victory, and the survivors, 105 in number, landed here, under the command of Captain Crozier." This paper was dated April 25,1848, and upon the following day they intended to start for the Great Fish River. The total loss by deaths in the expedition up to this date was nine officers and fifteen men. A vast quantity of clothing and stores of all sorts lay strewn about, as if here every article was thrown away which could possibly be dispensed with; pickaxes, shovels, boats, cooking utensils, ironwork, rope, blocks, canvas, a dip circle, a sextant engraved "Frederic Hornby, E.N.," a small medicine-chest, oars, &c. Lieutenant Hobson continued his search until within a few days' march of Cape Hersehell, without finding any trace of the wreck or of natives. He left full information of his important discoveries for me; therefore, when returning northward by the west shore of King William Island, I had the advantage of knowing what had already been found."

Another month passed as the men continued to find more and more evidence of the ultimate fate of Franklin's expedition. McClintock continued, "When we came to a large boat, discovered by Lieutenant Hobson a few days previously, as his notice informed me. It appears that this boat had been Intended for the ascent of the Fish River, but was abandoned apparently upon a return journey to the ships, the sledge upon which she was mounted being pointed in that direction. A large quantity of clothing was found within her, also two human skeletons. One of these lay in the after part of the boat, under a pile of clothing; the other, which was much more disturbed, probably by animals, was found in the bow. Five pocket watches, a quantity of silver spoons and forks, and a few religious books were also found, but no journals, pocket-books, or even names upon any articles of clothing. Two double-barrelled guns stood upright against the boat's side precisely as they had been placed 11 years before. One barrel in each was loaded and cocked; there was ammunition in abundance, also 30 lb. or 40 lb. of chocolate, some tea and tobacco. Fuel was not wanting; a drift tree lay within 100 yards of the boat. Many very interesting relics were brought away by Lieutenant Hobson, and some few by myself. On the 5th of June, I reached Point Victory without having found anything further. The clothing, &c., was again examined for documents, note-books, &c., without success, a record placed in the cairn, and another buried ten feet true north of it."

Having made its report, the *Times* went on to insist that any searches for more information be abandoned: "Franklin died more than twelve years ago. Since that day they have all shared the fate of their chief, dropping down one after another till the list man perished. Is there any sane man who will now propose that we should seek to enlarge the sphere of our knowledge, or that we should organise expeditions to find out the fate in detail of the 105 devoted men who, more than eleven years ago, set out, as we have reason to believe, from Point Victory for the Great Fish River? The lives of our gallant officers and men are dear to us all, but surely it is -wicked to expose that which we love to risk and loss to gratify a curiosity which deserves almost to be called morbid, in order to furnish us -with the exact particulars of the circumstances under which so many strong hearts and devoted souls were taken from us forever. No! England has surely now performed her mission. She has not, indeed, 'made war for an idea,' but she has offered up the noblest sacrifice even she could find on the altar of science."

The newspaper also put forth a thinly based criticism of the nation's ongoing search for the secret route to Asia, concluding, "It was not enough for her to know that the North-West Passage was closed by icy barriers against trade and commerce—it was not sufficient for her to leave the bleached bones of her children under solitary cairns in cold crusades against nature herself. She would hazard still more to identity every spot where her crusaders fell. We would fain follow, if it were of any use, the tramp of that noble band through the blinding snows and over the waste of iceberg and frozen sea, and pierce the gloom which must now for ever be the shroud in which they are enwrapped. We could find to-morrow sailors who would start off as cheerily on the search as ever Viking sailed from northern fiord to waste a southern isle, but the duty of Government is often graceless; it must often be in antagonism to the aspirations and desires of the government and here it is its duty, as it appears to us, to say, 'Let the dead bury their dead.' The report of Captain McClintock will close this sad eventful history. We must learn that there are yet powers in nature too strong for man to overcome. The dauntless soul dies out amid frost and snow; the spirit is never quenched though the body may perish. But what avails it all, if the physical obstacles remain the same forever, and leave to us only the barren glory of always lighting the fire which was extinguished? We retire now from the contest -with honour, if with grief, and we leave the name of Franklin engraved on the furthest pillars which the energy of mankind has dared to erect as the landmark of its research in the dull and useless region that guards the axis of the world."

Chapter 5: Solving the Mystery

Over 160 years after the crew disappeared, people continue to debate exactly what went wrong, and what set of circumstances conspired to take the lives of the crew. Together, scientists and historians have come up with a few theories. For instance, according to historian John Falkingham, Franklin made a critical error when he chose to go through Peel Sound to try to reach the Bering Strait, and through it, the Pacific Ocean. Unfortunately, he had no way of knowing that polar ice drifts down through the channel (ironically later named for McClintock) and piles clogs the sound. Falkingham explained, "To Franklin, [the path] would have been a very, very tempting route to take, particularly if it was open, free of ice. And Peel Sound, we know today, is very, very changeable from year to year. One year it can be completely wide open, another year it can be choked up with ice so that it's impassable even by modern ships. At the bottom end, at the south end of Peel Sound, is where he runs into that huge stream of Arctic Ocean polar ice. That is probably where he met his demise."

Based on this, Falkingham believes the ships remained trapped in ice for more than two years, with the ice never melting, until all their supplies ran out. "The nightmare scenario is that I'm never going to get out of this ice. I'm facing another long winter. It's going to get dark. It's going to get very cold. And here I am out on this ice that's still moving around. I don't know where this ice is carrying me."

Was it possible that the ice never melted that summer? To find out, a team of scientists led by Roy Koerner drilled down through more than 150 layers of ice to take a core sample from the time in which the Franklin party became trapped. He explained, "The reason ice cores give the history of the climate in the past is that everything that happens on the surface is preserved as the ice gets buried. If the surface of the snow melts, the water percolates down and it forms these ice layers. The more it melts the more ice layers and the thicker the ice layers. ... The point to make on this core is the absolute near absence of any signs of melting whatsoever, none of those clear layers at all. Just bubbly ice that is formed from compression of snow that doesn't melt in the summer. ... If it's a cold summer that ice isn't going to go out and open up. The channels are ice-infested still. The ships that they used in those days; they don't have the power to get through even modest ice."

Then there was the question most on Lady Franklin's mind. Again, 150 years later, more information finally emerged. Historian Russell Potter has observed, "It's amazing that we can tell this story at all. It's so fragmentary, the evidence so scattered. It's taken a tremendous amount of work; different people working in different disciplines to piece this puzzle together. And as we have done so, as the picture of what really happened has begun to emerge we've realized what they couldn't, and that's that they were basically doomed from the start. ... Ever since I first heard the Franklin story and just grasped the sense of the tragedy there, Beechey Island has been the magnet for me—the one place where you could stand and know that you were standing in Franklin's footsteps. ... They found signs that tents had been erected, a place where a smithy or anvil had been set up, even some attempt to build a garden up on the shingle."

Russell A. Potter's picture of crewmembers' graves on Beechey Island

Potter discovered evidence that Franklin and his men camped on Beechey Island in Nunavut, Canada, for more than six months. They found empty food cans, knives and other detritus, as well as the graves of three members of the party.

In 1984, scientists were given permission to exhume the bodies and found the surprise of their lives. John Geiger, who worked on the exhumation, recalled, "It was such a profoundly moving experience and also one of shock, really, or amazement, that these sailors from the last century—there they were. You could see their eye lashes you could see their eye color, you can get a sense almost of the personality of these characters. It's as if they had stepped forward in time to sort of answer very important questions that needed to be asked." In the end, he learned that the men, though young, had died of something rather prosaic, especially in the 19th century: tuberculosis. It seems that their damaged lungs, while perhaps strong enough to survive normal weather, was no match for the arctic cold.

The British would have undoubtedly preferred to keep their nation's failure a secret, but there were others in the world who were interested in the story and set out to investigate it. One of them was Charles Francis Hall, an American journalist who, in 1869, found Inuits who still recalled seeing Franklin and his team. Potter has examined his journals and insists, "Hall was just a very diligent man. He trusted the Inuit. He believed in their stories. He carefully corroborated one story with another to try to see how accurate that was likely to be. It matches very well with the physical evidence we have. It really is a highly accurate and amazingly well preserved oral tradition. They gave him a very vivid description of this place. They had seen tents on the land, bodies inside the tents, abandoned equipment."

Hall

The natives also described the men's appearances, referring specifically to their black skin and how even the insides of their mouths were black. The former is a symptom of frostbite, the latter of scurvy. Tragically, while Franklin had been sure that his men were provided with ample lemon juice to ward off the dreaded disease, he was unaware that the precious liquid loses its potency over time. As a result, by the third year of their mission, the illness was ravaging the men. Dr. Sundeep Dillon explains, "The first symptoms of scurvy are a sort of a general lassitude and a weakness and it mainly effects the gums. They become swollen, they become purple, the slightest touch means they bleed very, very easily. As it develops, the bleeding goes on everywhere, you can get bleeding into your eyes. You get bleeding into your muscles and this is particularly painful. The main muscle that you are using to try and pull this sled through the snow and you've got this agonizing bleeding into the muscles and into the joints, so it would have just slowly but horrendously killed them."

As if these symptoms were not bad enough, the men had another problem, one they could have known nothing about. Autopsies performed on exhumed skeletal remains showed evidence of serious lead poisoning. Anthropologist Anne Keenleyside noted, "They were so high that these individuals would have almost certainly been suffering from serious physiological and neurological problems. ... These individuals were exposed to this lead over a fairly recent period of time before their death. So this was short-term exposure, from some source on the expedition." Looking for a source of this poison, scientists examined the cans they had found at the site and discovered that they had been sealed with lead solder. In other words, the very rations that Franklin had been so proud of ultimately helped kill his men.

As the men became sicker, they also became more desperate. According to Potter, "It's clear from the Inuit testimony that at this point the traditional discipline is beginning to break down. The men are separating into different groups, possibly hostile to one another. Some are heading back to the ships, some camped on the land, some walking out by their own directions. None of them under the traditional central command that the Navy would expect. It's really the beginning of the end for them, everyone is trying to find their own solution. That breakdown in morale was starkly apparent from Inuit testimony describing an incident that took place on a one of the ship still trapped in the ice off the coast of King William Island."

Hall quoted an Inuit woman who told a frightening tale of the last days of some of the men: "The Inuit went to the ship all alone. He said there were men there. He said they had black faces, black hands, black clothes on, were black all over. This Inuit was very alarmed because they would not let him get away. Then a captain came out of the cabin and put a stop to it. Then the Captain took this Inuit down with him into his cabin. He told him to look over to the land where there are men living in a big tent. He said neither the Inuit nor any of his people must ever go there."

More than 150 years passed before anyone outside the party itself knew why the natives were told not to go there. After examining bone fragments found on King William Island in 1994, Keenleyside answered the lingering question: "We saw very distinct cut marks. These were quite different from animal tooth marks. These look like very definite cut marks as if they were made by some kind of a knife or metal blade. ... A lot of the cuts were located in the vicinity of the joints. Some of the bones that would have been covered by a lot of flesh or soft tissue. We also found cuts, interestingly, in the bones of the hands and feet. And the hands and the feet are probably the most human aspects of the body apart from the face. And the fact that we were finding cuts in those locations suggested to me that perhaps these individuals were intentionally removing those more human aspects of the body. I think this evidence is strongly suggestive of cannibalism among these Franklin crewmembers. I don't see any other possible explanation that would account for those cut marks." As a result, the worst case scenario was confirmed: the men had indeed resorted to eating the frozen remains of their fallen comrades.

With her husband's death confirmed, it might have made sense that Lady Franklin would no longer sponsor Arctic expeditions, but this was not the case. In 1874, the *London Globe* reported, "The Pandora, which was one of the vessels named for the Arctic expedition, but was condemned on survey, has been purchased from the Admiralty by Mr. Allen Young, a lieutenant in the Royal Naval Reserve, who will assume command of her…. Mr. Young served with Admiral Sir Leopold McClintock on board the Fox in the Franklin Search expedition, and it is stated that the expense of fliting out the Pandora will now be borne by Lady Franklin and Mr. Gordon Bennett, of the New York Herald."

Unfortunately, many of the same problems that plagued Franklin's party ended up stopping Young before he could reach the last known location of the failed expedition. On October 25, 1875, *The Magnet, Agricultural, Commercial, And Family Gazette* in London reported, "No little surprise was manifested at Portsmouth on Sunday on it becoming known that the Pandora sloop, Capt. Allen Young, had returned from her voyage of discovery, on which she set out from here only about three months and a half since. The Pandora…was fitted out in the spring at Southampton, where an extra 41.5 inches of American elm was added to her, thus making her admirably adapted for serving in the Arctic Seas. Everything was done on board to make her as snug as possible, and she left port on the 28th of July with very fair hopes of achieving the object in view—that of entering the Polar Circle, and going through the North-west Passage. Off Cape Farewell and on the way up Waigat Strait, some Spitsbergen ice was met with."

The article continued by laying out the details of the expedition's attempt to find Franklin's last location: "On Aug. 13 a start was made from Upernivik, and the Pandora proceeded across Melville Bay, which was found quite clear of ice. The north-west island of the Carey group was reached on the 13th of August, and a party having been sent ashore three cairns were found, all of which, however, were empty, the supposition being that they had been used by whalers. On the 20th of August the entrance of Lancaster Sound was reached, and no little difficulty was experienced in passing the pack ice which was met off Cape Warrender, the pack being something like fifty miles wide. The Pandora was then steered for Beechy Island, situated about 74 deg. N. off which they arrived on the evening of the 26th. … Leaving Beechy Island, the course of the Pandora was steered for Peel Straits, where she arrived on the evening of the 28th, where they were again stopped by the pack. The Pandora had to moor to the ice for a week, during which time the officers were on it and had some seal shooting, several seals being killed. After cruising about for some little time, an opening was discovered on the southern shore, and the Pandora went through as far as Limestone Island, where a cairn was erected and records left. After a good deal of difficulty, the Pandora succeeded in passing the pack, and working through Limestone Island, where signs of open waters were first met with."

Though they were out of danger for the moment, Young and his men soon realized there was little else they could do and decided to return home. The article concluded, "Navigation in that portion of the Arctic seas is exceedingly difficult, and bumps and knocks from the ice were by no means rare, though, fortunately, no injury was occasioned to the Pandora. On the 29th, the farthest point reached by the Fox was passed when she tried to reach King William's Land, and here the Pandora found open water. On the 30th Laronette and Bellot Island were reached. Off that little place her progress was completely stopped by an impassable pack of ice from twenty to thirty feet thick and as solid as granite. After beating about for three days, it was decided, as no possible advantage could be gained by wintering in that spot, to turn the Pandora's head and return home, first going back to Carey Islands to make a fuller search for records left by Captain Nares. The pack which provide too formidable for the Pandora was the same which caused the Fox to turn back, penetrate it. The Pandora passed Cape Farewell on the 3rd Oct. Two days after they were overtaken by a terrible N.W. gale, the fiercest Capt. Young remembers, and the Pandora scudded along before it at a tremendous rate, until within a short distance of the English Channel. One sea pooped the Pandora, but. no damage was done. Off Cape Horsburg four bears were killed, and a fine cub was captured by Lieut. Brie with a lasso; it has been brought home, as well as four Esquimaux dogs. It is believed to be the intention of Captain Young to start again far the Arctic next year, but much earlier."

While Young did return to the Arctic, it was not to look for Franklin. In fact, there were no other serious searches for the lost crew, just as there were no more serious attempts to reach Asia by sailing west. In the end, England finally decided that it had wasted enough lives on what proved to be a (very clogged) pipe dream, and it has been left to a member of the British Commonwealth, Canada, to safeguard the final resting places of the two legendary ships.

A depiction of *Terror* caught in ice in the Arctic

Online Resources

Other British history titles by Charles River Editors

Other titles about explorers and expeditions by Charles River Editors

Other Franklin expedition titles on Amazon

Bibliography

Beardsley, Martin (2002). *Deadly Winter: The Life of Sir John Franklin*. London: Chatham Publishing.

Beattie, Owen & Geiger, John (1987). Frozen in Time: Unlocking the Secrets of the Franklin Expedition. Saskatoon: Western Producer Prairie Books.

Brandt, Anthony (2010). The Man Who Ate His Boots: The Tragic History of the Search for the Northwest Passage.

Brown, John, F.R.G.S. (1860). The North-West Passage and the Plans for the Search for Sir John Franklin: A Review with maps, &c., Second Edition with a Sequel Including the Voyage of the Fox. London: Edward Stanford.

Cookman, Scott (2000). *Iceblink: The Tragic Fate of Sir John Franklin's Lost Polar Expedition*. New York: John Wiley & Sons.

Cyriax, Richard (1939). *Sir John Franklin's Last Arctic Expedition; a Chapter in the History of the Royal Navy*. London: Methuen & Co.

Davis-Fisch, Heather (2012). *Loss and Cultural Remains in Performance: The Ghosts of the Franklin Expedition*. Toronto: Palgrave Macmillan.

Lambert, Andrew (2010). *Franklin: Tragic Hero of Polar Exploration*. London: Faber and Faber.

M'Clintock, Francis L. (1860). *The Voyage of the Fox in the Arctic Seas: A Narrative of the Discovery of the Fate of Sir John Franklin and His Companions*. Boston: Ticknor and Fields.

Sandler, Martin (2006). *Resolute: The Epic Search for the Northwest Passage and John Franklin, and the Discovery of the Queen's Ghost Ship*. New York: Sterling Publishing Co.

Schwatka, Frederick (1965). Edouard A. Stackpole, ed. *The Long Arctic Search; the Narrative of Lieutenant Frederick Schwatka, U.S.A., 1878–1880, Seeking the Records of the Lost Franklin Expedition*. New Bedford, Massachusetts: Reynolds-DeWalt.

Woodman, David C. (1992). *Unravelling the Franklin Mystery: Inuit Testimony*. Montreal: McGill-Queen's University Press.

Free Books by Charles River Editors

We have brand new titles available for free most days of the week. To see which of our titles are currently free, click on this link.

Discounted Books by Charles River Editors

We have titles at a discount price of just 99 cents everyday. To see which of our titles are currently 99 cents, click on this link.

CPSIA information can be obtained
at www.ICGtesting.com
Printed in the USA
LVOW10s1018230417
531866LV00019B/474/P